THE OPPOSITE OF CLAUSTROPHOBIA

Prime's Anti-Autobiography

Eileen R. Tabios

NEWTON-LE-WILLOWS

Published in the United Kingdom in 2017
by The Knives Forks And Spoons Press,
122 Birley Street,
Newton-le-Willows,
Merseyside,
WA12 9UN.

ISBN 978-1-909443-88-4

Copyright Eileen R. Tabios, 2017.

The right of Eileen R. Tabios to be identified as the author of this work has been asserted by her in accordance with the Copyrights, Designs and Patents Act of 1988. All rights reserved. No part of this publication may be reproduced, stored in a retrieval system, transmitted in any form or by any means, electronic, photocopying, recording or otherwise, without prior permission of the publisher.

ACKNOWLEDGEMENTS:

Excerpts of this poem were first published in *Marsh Hawk Review* (2015), Editor Norman Finkelstein; *X-Peri* (2016), Editor Daniel Y. Harris; and my earlier book *INVENT(ST)ORY: Selected Catalog Poems & New 1996-2015* (Dos Madres Press, 2015), Editor/Publisher Robert Murphy. My gratitude to the editors.

Cover Image: "Prime" (Drawing, 2016) by Nico Vassilakis

*For Achilles, Gabriela, Athena & Ajax,
because "Dogs are Pure Love"*

PRIME

2	3	5	7	11	13	17
19	23	29	31	37	41	43
47	53	59	61	67	71	73
79	83	89	97	101	103	107
109	113	127	131	137	139	149
151	157	163	167	173	179	181
191	193	197	199	211	223	227
229	233	239	241	251	257	263
269	271	277	281	283	293	307
311	313	317	331	337	347	349
353	359	367	373	379	383	389
397	401	409	419	421	431	433
439	443	449	457	461	463	467
479	487	491	499	503	509	521
523	541	547	557	563	569	571
577	587	593	599	601	607	613
617	619	631	641	643	647	653
659	661	673	677	683	691	701
709	719	727	733	739	743	751
757	761	769	773	787	797	809
811	821	823	827	829	839	853
857	859	863	877	881	883	887
907	911	919	929	937	941	947
953	967	971	977	983	991	997
1,009	1,013	1,019	1,021	1,031	1,033	1,039
1,049	1,051	1,061	1,063	1,069	1,087	1,091
1,093	1,097	1,103	1,109	1,117	1,123	1,129
1,151	1,153	1,163	...	...	...	...

I forgot I knew the back alleys of this neighbourhood, where beggars made their beds, whose cats stole their food, which doorways provided for or grabbed the fragile into a clench of cruelty.

I forgot why lovers destroy children to parse the philosophy of separation.

I forgot how quickly civilization can disappear, as swiftly as the shoreline from an oil spill birthed from a twist of the wrist by a drunk vomiting over the helm.

I forgot the horizon is far, is near, is what you wish but always in front of you.

I forgot how your eyes always reached for me when I passed the threshold into the home we carefully shared.

I forgot grabbing at my fading dreams only to recall a vision of skyscrapers crumbling from the slaps of iron balls.

I forgot there are no guarantees, not even in math where "1 + 1" may not be "2" but, as a visual artist insisted, "11" or, as a philosopher insisted, "a turning towards the other."

I forgot memory's fragments which deserve to be the ones in the forefront of my attention.

I forgot how, like a cabdriver with his first
ride after hours of scouring emptied streets,
he needed to speak.

I forgot how his grin pushed away the gloom
of a spent lightbulb hovering in the dimness
we shared.

I forgot my hope he would speak of me to his
friend who became a stranger after so many
neighbourly greetings in elevator rides from a
past we shared before a certain diagnosis:
"HIV-Positive."

I forgot missing teeth and gums full of potholes.

I forgot my mistake. The radically old and the radically young are the same in their difference from me—they do not need much, they need too much. They do not ask, they must often plead. I forgot how, unlike them, I knew what it took to survive.

I forgot that to return bore no relationship to survival, which instead related to you whose path crossed mine in a new land.

I forgot the mud in monsoon season always sucked at the ankles, non-discriminating, a placid surface but camouflaging sharply-edged stones, gooooey, gooooey, gooooey and brown as the hide on rotten bananas.

I forgot how my mother vainly searched for mangos when she would visit during the wrong season.

I forgot the grandfather who willingly faced a fire, fist trembling at the indifferent sky.

I forgot the elders, shoulders sagged to ruin, dropping gazes like debris and treasuring trees for their shade that exacts no price.

I forgot abandoning misery until it became mere concept, then poem.

I forgot the mud like the skin of my grandmother, her gum-teethed cronies and other wiry residents of a patient village beaten by the sun.

I forgot mangoes, eaten before they ripened – they were savoured with much salt and first soaked in vinegar.

I forgot a neighbour who stole my pet pig and ate the evidence.

I forgot it need not take more than one person to bring the world to ruin – for my mother, that person was me.

I forgot entrancement with the layered auras of decay.

I forgot I began drowning in air.

I forgot the night was unanimous.

I forgot how one begins marking time from a lover's utterance of Farewell.

I forgot one can use colour to prevent encounters from degenerating into lies.

I forgot I was not an immigrant; I was simply myself who lacked control at how the world formed outside the "Other" of me.

I forgot admiring women who refuse to paint their lips.

I forgot the liberating anonymity conferred by travel: *Mindanao, Berlin, Melbourne, Amsterdam, Istanbul* became hours requiring no count.

I forgot obviating memory for what I believed was a higher purpose.

I forgot feeling you in the air against my cheek.

I forgot longing for a sky without horizon, but acceding instead to the eye's clamour against the opposite of claustrophobia.

I forgot you thought of me as you paced the streets of a city whose sidewalks memorised the music of my footsteps dancing away from youth into courage.

I forgot I lit alleys by leaving scarlet roses whose perfume, I hoped, you would discern.

I forgot you saw each virgin moon as a ruby you wanted for adorning my body.

I forgot you startled the girl whose poetry elicits dragon scales from empathetic muscles.

I forgot England with its glazed chintzes
bearing sprays of rose, peony, hydrangea
and gladiola – names evoking country
houses: *Bowood, Amberley, Sissinghurst,
Sutherland.*

I forgot the rest of Greece, its national heat
waiting.

I forgot you falling asleep in my skin to
dream.

I forgot, for him, she released milk to orphaned baby birds.

I forgot the flock with tin feathers.

I forgot an island replete with chastened alleyways.

I forgot Burkina Faso.

I forgot gardenias were crushed for perfume entrusted with canceling midnights.

I forgot where bones erupted mountains in Guatemala and Peru.

I forgot radiance must penetrate if it is to caress, and its price can never reach blasphemy.

I forgot the fraying edges of fabrics still mustering to cover the shoulders of non-retired warriors.

I forgot we, together, formed tuning forks longing for empathetic hits.

I forgot painting a floor red with my hair. I forgot backing myself into a corner: when you appeared to grasp my throat, your greedy footprints completed my painting.

I forgot how one can sag into night as if night was a lover.

I forgot a lake capitulating with ripples from a stone's impassive penetration.

I forgot the compromise of writing *typhoid fever* as falsely synonymous with ecstasy. I forgot writing *typhoid fever* as manifesting the sublime.

I forgot I could not forget the hollow cheeks
on mothers cradling dead warriors.

I forgot nights lactating morphine, roses
rebelling against the aftermath of blooming,
and the vampires about to sin.

I forgot Marisa peeling the skin from a blue-
boned fish, Shakira rustling up an old
clothesline for tying hands together after
mosquitoes bit, Doris with ears attuned to
lullabies emanating from the wings of
fireflies, Luisa who squatted besides betel-
chewing crones with crooked front teeth, and
Marjorie who swallowed the scarless sky
over Siquijor.

I forgot a set of instructions that ended with the order, *Do not cry.*

I forgot you spilling vermouth on the sky.

I forgot my son flinging his leather jacket over a puddle intersecting with my path across Bluemner Street.

I forgot the "Ideal Violet" whose petals blush during the lemonade days of summer.

I forgot that if you call an island "Isla Mujeres," half of the population will be anguished.

I forgot psoriasis enabling disparagement.

I forgot powwows without credibility.

I forgot the gravestone outmanoeuvres all.

I forgot you turned time into eternity by waiting at the gate.

I forgot Lexus engineers.

I forgot Las Vegas' invitation to be at home with The Topless The Wet, The White: *Mandalay Bay!*

I forgot gifts carefully differentiated among recipients – the matron's painstaking definitions of servants versus those served.

I forgot ~~the difficulty in dying~~ the world saw me as a hunchback.

I forgot drinking from ancient goblets whose cracked rims snagged lips into a bleeding burning. I forgot my skin was ruin.

I forgot a girl shrieking as her swing soared towards a boiling sky.

I forgot "abashed aubergine."

I forgot cheer dispersed through fishnet stockings.

I forgot the skin of jasmine mirroring sky.

I forgot the empress humming calculus.

I forgot the air of a country where the love for a woman is the love for a man is the love for Allah!

I forgot to freeze the spiral that is memory's perspective.

I forgot pepper as the visual substitute for truffles.

I forgot the scent of a lunatic negative.

I forgot the ember of amber.

I forgot the pleasurable tension of avidity.

I forgot sausage fat sizzling with the passion of cultists.

I forgot molasses.

I forgot ice relaxing its contours into liquid gold.

I forgot the deceit in conclusions.

I forgot the seams caused by bindings.

I forgot fringes.

I forgot a wave of grasshoppers blocking the view of a headless Buddha.

I forgot meagre pity.

I forgot omission as confession.

I forgot dungeons waste marble.

I forgot that *piccola città* replete with hyphens.

I forgot minarets growing within muddy whirlpools.

I forgot kohl telling stories without words.

I forgot her hobby of attending to death beds – afterwards, she always lusted for hotel lobbies stuffed with crystal chandeliers.

I forgot the perfume of fresh bread outside a *panetteria*, the vinegary tang floating from a wine shop, heaven as the scent of roasting coffee from a grocer, and the necessary reminder of those different from us through the stench of street drains.

I forgot fallen olives discarded from those awaiting virgin pressings.

I forgot sighting a bloodied face through a cracked windshield, and moving on.

I forgot too many hot and dusty evenings at train stations.

I forgot a limp laundry line, almost invisible in the grey air.

I forgot injected air bubbles.

I forgot instructing saliva to wait.

I forgot she quivered like 19th century theatre.

I forgot turning professorial with a box of Corona Gordas harrumphing by my side.

I forgot her interior became an effective compass.

I forgot lies crafting incentives.

I forgot a dungeon's red velvet chair crashing to its side so that our pens would mate.

I forgot I opened the Iron Gate for you by losing wings – *o lost shields for my eyes tracking an old target: the Sun!*

I forgot my father is not Idi Amin of Uganda.

I forgot my father is not Nicolae Ceausescu of Romania.

I forgot my father is not Francisco Franco Bahamonde of Spain.

I forgot my father is not Joseph Goebbels of Germany.

I forgot my father is not Kim Il Sung of North Korea.

I forgot my father is not Anastasio Somoza of Nicaragua.

I forgot my father is not Mohamed Suharto of Indonesia.

I forgot my father is not and never has been a president of the United States:
    Harry S. Truman
    Dwight D. Eisenhower
    John F. Kennedy
    Lyndon B. Johnson
    Richard M. Nixon

Gerald Ford
Jimmy Carter
Ronald Reagan
George Bush
Bill Clinton
George W. Bush
Barack Obama

I forgot music became a jail.

I forgot waiting for Etel Adnan's new form of absence: "exile from exile."

I forgot what was never called by a name.

I forgot flamenco's Third Commandment: never reveal ... to outsiders.

I forgot green mornings pulsing with the ferocious flowers of red hearts.

I forgot draping black velvet over the sun.

I forgot Clementina laughing at her bruises, both then and those yet to come.

I forgot joining gypsies to adore Juana specifically for her madness.

I forgot how effectively pain obviates abstractions.

I forgot we agreed to toss away the blindfold so that our ears can become more than holes for burning stones tossed our way by a cruel race.

I forgot flying fish are always wide-eyed always breathless always look unbelieving.

I forgot the chill of kissing the wrong man. *O lifetime of pearls!*

I forgot I refused to smash a bagpipe. I anticipated and was always afraid of the image of a discarded lung atop the asphalt of your aborted road.

I forgot how a stairway muffled but still sang our song.

I forgot how, when they heard the Singer, they heard a man jailed for stealing a bunch of grapes, then the ugly grunts of his starving children.

I forgot I learned to stamp my heels to sound a machine-gun blast. I forgot I didn't need a man to bring me fire so I can forge a song.

I forgot to live like Lorca and Loca with the voice of a nightingale, a bullet in its breast.

I forgot the musk of evenings quivering into post-elegance.

I forgot there was no need to apologise for
dancing from one's hips roundly, eyes
closed, taking up as much space as one
wanted on the dance floor of someone else's
wedding.

I forgot three coyotes peeing upon the
buttercups.

I forgot the hunched sommelier correcting,
"You mean 'saddle leather'," thus learning
one can forget what one never knew.

I forgot the "wet jade" eyes of cats can make you forget felines are always dusty.

I forgot a wall at dusk whose shelves of books turned their backs for their spines to stare at you as a neighbour's saxophone elongated.

I forgot a sepia photograph slipping from brittle pages.

I forgot believing the world was populated by the hearts of mothers who would always welcome back prodigal sons and daughters with warm rice and cold slices of pineapple.

The Opposite of Claustrophobia

I forgot a sarong fell and a river blushed.

I forgot a stone garden in Kyoto where the 15th stone is invisible from all angles.

I forgot you living somewhere along my spine. I forgot integral yoga to squeeze you more efficiently out of bone marrow.

I forgot a girl singing, *I will become Babaylan!* with notes only virgin boys can muster, only dogs can hear.

I forgot a girl singing as she smooched the sun …

I forgot there are keys to everything, even handcuffs missing their rabbit fur linings.

I forgot disappointing myself for emulating Lucan who created *Bellum Civile* by using Vergil's *Aeneid* as a "negative compositional model."

I forgot the hundreds of words in Hindi that mean "lotus."

I forgot she tottered on ice despite thick ankles.

I forgot penury forcing me into a staring contest with an ice cube.

I forgot Catullus due to his scurrilous invective.

I forgot a desecrated battleground as a condition precedent towards becoming an artist.

I forgot I saw a city bleeding beyond the window and felt Manila's infamously red sunset staining street children whose hopes concerned absolutely no one.

I forgot stepping on pine cones and ensuring my smile never slipped.

I forgot the trip wire leering as it hid in the shimmer of summer heat.

I forgot experiencing wine and its cousins so I could address what I could not control. I forgot how, later, the same experience became a fabric my memory crafted into a shimmering silver ballgown because I accepted discipline.

I forgot a "Mom" and "Dad" bringing me to a turquoise house cheered by kittens and where I learned meals will be finished and still there will be food for the next.

I forgot the lucidity of ancient mountains.

I forgot a carapace, then its splitting.

I forgot how, afterwards, I always turned away as if the wall would not only speak but console.

I forgot you understood immediately what would require months of your meticulously loving mockery, at times harsh and at times subtle, for me to learn I forgot how swiftly you pushed us to begin.

I forgot yet another cliché – how I came to consider anew the significance of a scarf
as it tears
as it ties
as it muffles
as it falls
as it knots
as it hides
as it binds
as its colours fade despite the absence of light deep within a locked closet.

I forgot the Sphinx's unasked riddle:
    "Which is more powerful?
    A moon so bright it erases night
    or
    A sun so bright it darkens vision?"

I forgot that a painting fails when it images the fall of an apple instead of the shattered aftermath, or survival within an unexpected catch-and-hold.

I forgot that I memorised your one published biography. Today I went to the library to read it again. But it was not available. Someone else was reading your story.

I forgot you cradled me.

I forgot because I thought it best to forget everything rather than remember schemes informed by my desire rather than what actually transpired.

I forgot the mysterious Chinese who slipped syphilis to Vincent Van Gogh – she was a refugee from something unknown thus only imaginable by us: a world of people with hacked-off hands, thus, no paintings to criticise or admire.

I forgot how to perceive with tenderness.

I forgot the alley of your city where I stood as a statue frozen by unrequited longing.

I forgot Arthur Rimbaud who said the bears are dancing but what we had wanted to do was move the stars to pity.

I forgot Eric Gill's fascination with the sexual organs of animals – he peered through microscopes to compare a cow's semen with his own.

I forgot the dwarf Henri de Toulouse-Lautrec defining paradise as "a world of female odours and nerve endings."

I forgot the collapse of New York City
towers – I forgot inhaling their spines to
become mine in the aftermath.

I forgot the blades of Army helicopters slicing air into thinner and thinner strips.

I forgot the grandmother who was too old to run.

I forgot the estimate of orphans worldwide is inherently a square root.

I forgot the opposite of fog.

I forgot the reeds were frozen *into* it because the river was entirely frozen.

I forgot they were born into a dowerless present.

I forgot battling priests as I re-educated a child into learning consequences occur before any after-life.

I forgot that meditation, if conducted deeply, must harvest pain.

I forgot the wet walls of a beer bottle, against which I had laid my brow.

I forgot how I went through a phase at poetry readings of ripping pages from my books – sometimes I'd autograph them before handing them out with a *"They're worthy of Ebay!"* Sometimes I crumpled them into balls I'd toss towards the audience as if they were money or my underwear.

I forgot space is difficult to depict without the negative grid.

I forgot a poem with multiple references that became whole through a scaffolding of jazz.

I forgot the dictator who was my father.

I forgot the timidity of your sixth toe.

ABOUT THE POET:

Eileen R. Tabios loves books and has released about 40 collections of poetry, fiction, essays, and experimental biographies from publishers in nine countries and cyberspace. Recipient of the Philippines' National Book Award for Poetry for her first poetry collection, she has seen her poems translated into eight languages as well as inspire collaborations involving computer-generated hybrid languages, paintings, video, kali martial marts, modern dance, among others. She also has edited, co-edited or conceptualised ten anthologies of poetry, fiction and essays as well as served as editor or guest editor for various literary journals. Inventor of the poetic form "hay(na)ku," she maintains a biblioliphic blog, "Eileen Verbs Books"; edits *Galatea Resurrects*, a popular poetry review; steers the literary and arts publisher Meritage Press; and curates thematic online poetry projects including *LinkedIn Poetry Recommendations* (a recommended list of contemporary poetry books). After releasing a collection of short novels, she is currently writing a long-form novel. More information is available at http://eileenrtabios.com

PREVIOUSLY BY EILEEN R. TABIOS

POETRY

After The Egyptians Determined The Shape of the World is a Circle, 1996
Beyond Life Sentences, 1998
The Empty Flagpole (CD with guest artist Mei-mei Berssenbrugge), 2000
Ecstatic Mutations, 2001 (with short stories and essays)
Reproductions of The Empty Flagpole, 2002
Enheduanna in the 21st Century, 2002
There, Where the Pages Would End, 2003
Menage a Trois With the 21st Century, 2004
Crucial Bliss Epilogues, 2004
The Estrus Gaze(s), 2005
SONGS OF THE COLON, 2005
POST BLING BLING, 2005
I Take Thee, English, For My Beloved, 2005
The Secret Lives of Punctuations, Vol. I, 2006
Dredging for Atlantis, 2006
It's Curtains, 2006
SILENCES: The Autobiography of Loss, 2007
The Singer and Others: Flamenco Hay(na)ku, 2007
The Light Sang As It Left Your Eyes: Our Autobiography, 2007
NOTA BENE EISWEIN, 2009
Footnotes to Algebra: Uncollected Poems 1995-2009, 2009
Roman Holiday, 2010
THE THORN ROSARY: Selected Prose Poems and New 1998-2010, 2010
the relational elations of ORPHANED ALGEBRA (with j/j hastain), 2012
5 Shades of Gray, 2012
THE AWAKENING: A Long Poem Triptych & A Poetics Fragment, 2013

147 MILLION ORPHANS (MMXI-MML), 2014
44 RESURRECTIONS, 2014
SUN STIGMATA (Sculpture Poems), 2014
I FORGOT LIGHT BURNS, 2015
DUENDE IN THE ALLEYS, 2015
INVENT(ST)ORY: SELECTED CATALOG POEMS & NEW (1996–2015), 2015
THE CONNOISSEUR OF ALLEYS, 2016
The Gilded Age of Kickstarters, 2016
AMNESIA: Somebody's Memoir, 2016
EXCAVATING THE FILIPINO IN ME, 2016
THE OPPOSITE OF CLAUSTROPHOBIA: Prime's Anti-Autobiography, 2017

FICTION

Behind The Blue Canvas, 2004
SILK EGG: Collected Novels 2009-2009, 2011

PROSE COLLECTIONS

Black Lightning, 1998 (poetry essays/interviews)
My Romance, 2002 (art essays with poems)
The Blind Chatelaine's Keys, 2008 (biography with haybun)

www.ingramcontent.com/pod-product-compliance
Lightning Source LLC
Chambersburg PA
CBHW051702040426
42446CB00009B/1261